Roman Fischer

Rules to Rule Successfully!

Table of Contents

Introduction

Imagine that you have begun planning for the future: you are determined to drop your mediocrity and become someone special. That means no more excuses and hiding behind the self-serving phrases 'could have, should have, would have.'

Instead, you're taking action to release your full potential to the outside world. It's time to stop worrying and start living. You will no longer allow fear to bring you to your knees. Not at all.

The first things you will have to cope with are rules, rules, rules. Nobody likes them. Many consider them a ball and chain and a straightjacket designed to take away your freedom. Right? Well, not exactly. While rules do restrict you, they are intended to help you become a better person. If more people would apply even a few good rules to their life, then they would gradually notice a positive change.

You can select which rules you will follow, how many, and when you want to follow them. However, if you opt for no rules at all to live by then life will be chaotic and completely unstructured -- and structure is what helps mold you into a better and more successful person. Once your life structure is in place you need to remain faithful to your goal, without undue influence. And you must always believe in yourself, as cliché as this may sound. Success doesn't come easily and it most certainly doesn't come to those who are not steadfast. It's as simple as this: to get what you want you need to GO AFTER it with vigor.

It's also a good rule of thumb to be patient because as the saying goes, "good things come to those who wait." Rarely if ever do people bask in the limelight without first enduring the grind of waiting patiently for what they want. You must mentally prepare yourself with the help of set rules for the difficult road ahead of you. Without this guidance, you will be traveling in the wilderness and greatly diminish your chances of success.

Ultimately, it is your goal that will determine how hard and how often you will need to work.

Oftentimes, people give up far too early without realizing that they are so close to their goal. There is always light at the end of the tunnel so don't stop and ponder in the darkness too long, or it will swallow you and then you will become the insignificant person that you never wanted to be. Strive for more, dream bigger, keep your expectations set incredibly high on achievements, and most of all, follow certain rules closely to ensure that you will become a better, more successful person in the long run.

Rule #1: Plan for What's yet to Come

If you just live for today and don't ever think about tomorrow, then chances are you will be surprised with dissatisfaction. It's like having a goal to lose ten pounds but no plan how you will do it. The key is to have a set goal to keep yourself on course. Just like humans need rules to ensure a safe and functional society, you also need to have set plans for yourself to achieve those things for which you have always yearned.

Planning ahead offers so many benefits. It helps make things cheaper in some cases, it allows you to have less stress in your everyday life, and much more. While it's of course a great idea to also enjoy your life right now and the journey towards your goals, you should never forget to have at least a couple of well-planned goals for your future. Goal setting is suitable for everybody, and don't think you're ever too old to set some awesome expectations for yourself! It's good to be realistic, however, you don't want them to be too realistic as that sometimes leads towards mediocrity. Remember your goal is to escape remaining your old "just average" person.

While you're goal-planning, make sure to consider how long it takes and how long you're actually willing to wait. Naturally, the more complex your dream, the longer it will take to reach. If you want to be more than average, then be prepared to wait longer. Many successful people waited years before they obtained their big break. Some achieved their success in their twenties, thirties, or even much later. It's never too late for you! If you plan on going to college after high school, plan on becoming a doctor after college, or whatever your intention is you need to think before taking action. Of course, doing so too quickly and just making a specific decision in a situation simply on spontaneity is one of the worst things you could do. You need to lock your focus on what you love and pursue that. Avoid regrets and always seize the opportunity before it vanishes.

Decision making is definitely critical for a triumphant future. Without the proper planning, you can ultimately get yourself in a rut and it can get pretty ugly. Remember to also not pursue an area just because your friends are. You are your own person and you should have a mind of your own. It pays to be independent. You do NOT want or need somebody breathing down your neck every step of the way. With more money and time gained by planning ahead, you will have more options. If you ever don't like what you're currently doing, then you can simply change it. Typically, it can be a challenge to change your career because you will probably find yourself scrambling for time. However, since planning ahead is so beneficial you will have more of a 'rebound-time' than others.

Being a prosperous person is about getting ahead while you compete with others. Fortunately, for pre-planners many aren't willing to go that extra mile. With this being the case, you can easily set yourself apart from others practically by the snap of a finger. All this "never give up" and "plan ahead" talk has definitely been corny for the longest time, but it works. It's easier said than done, but you need to do whatever it takes to make you happy. If you aren't happy then you are doing something wrong. Ditto if you aren't struggling. Well...usually when you don't struggle nothing beneficial will happen.

Another sweet perk of planning for the future that many don't notice is that you will be less likely to give up. With the 'rebound-time' you earn by arranging for the future, you will become more confident in knowing that your dream could just become a reality as everything will be more stable. It may not necessarily be a sudden reality, but it could happen and that's all you need. Just knowing that your dream can become a reality produces hope and that makes life much easier.

Not to mention, with your future more assured because of preparation, you will be mentally healthier. In turn, this will increase your chances of living a longer and higher quality of life. This will lead to being socially healthier as you will be a more pleasant person; you will smile more, laugh more, etc. Physically you will also be better off because you won't have all the worries of not knowing what to expect next. Thus, you will age slower. Let's say you wanted to look good and youthful for a photoshoot for school pictures or for a modeling gig, well, if you plan for what's yet to come then you won't worry as often and as a result, wrinkles and other unwanted aging features won't show up as quickly as others who do worry. These are just some of the countless advantages of planning for your future! So, plan soon and plan well!

Rule #2: Don't Let Failure Consume You

Have you ever failed miserably at something? Maybe the right thing to ask is: did you ever give up on what you were seeking to attain? You see, you only fail when you give up. Of course, you can make mistakes in situations, but that isn't a real failure. Once you make a mistake there is always room to correct it and better yourself. Just as fear strains people's hope of succeeding so does failure. Failure and fear often pair with each other. In all actuality, they don't have to worry about failing unless they just chose to quit once and for all.

As soon as you get out of bed in the morning, the mentality you should have is that it doesn't matter where you stumble because you are a work in progress. You constantly will make errors, but you will constantly have room to fix them and start anew. Life was never easy nor fair and there's absolutely no way you can expect to progress successfully without a stable, healthy mindset. You don't want to have an idle mind because as you already know, an idle mind is a devil's workshop. Too much down time could very well let your mind start feeding you negative thoughts. It's necessary to get occupied with activities as much as possible (whether it be: basketball, soccer, swimming, shopping, etc.) to counteract any possible pessimistic thoughts.

Not only is too much down time a bad thing, but it is also an ugly thing. If you never take breaks from pursuing your dreams, you will likely be overwhelmed and exhausted. You'll find that a lot of your time was too focused on one thing and not on other stuff. Time is precious and should be spent wisely. Just because something you go after doesn't work for you right away doesn't mean you should quit, but it also doesn't mean that you should obsess about it. Keep in mind that when you go out places you can gain friends, but also haters too who will criticize every move you make. If your haters knew that you could walk on water, then they would say that you couldn't swim. Basically, no matter what you do you will always meet haters who can't be pleased because haters are...well they're just haters. You can't expect to please everybody. It's impossible and a waste of time and energy.

You need to please yourself, that's truly what matters. Don't fixate on other people's opinions.

When you succeed or fail at something, you will typically get feedback. It may be good or bad depending on how well you did. Assuming you mess up at what you were working at, you will then get some kind of criticism. There's two types of criticism: constructive and just plain old criticism. Taking constructive criticism now and then is beneficial, but not pure criticism. Know that there's a difference between the two. One will help you improve your life and the other could take a toll on you emotionally. Once you stop listening to all the negative comments directed at you, you can then finally focus on the most important one: your own.

Learn to first forgive yourself before you begin to love yourself. Without accepting your past and present flaws you will never truly be happy with who you are, thus making it impossible for you to love yourself. It's also wise to take into account that you will, without a doubt, have future flaws. Understanding this will help brace yourself for your future which will, at times, be very unsteady.

Once you attain self-acceptance, then and only then will you be able to start working towards your passion. Believe it or not, another way to strengthen your confidence and pride is to do some form of work like chores for instance. More than likely, it's not what you wanted to hear, but sometimes doing tiring tasks could make you feel accomplished. There's just a strong sense of pride that will radiate from inside you after you accomplish even the simplest of tasks. Maybe do easy tasks like taking out the trash or loading dishes. If you want an even stronger sense of pride, then mow the lawn or any other yard work.

Of course, it's good to note that you can also become overconfident and prideful. While it's wonderful to feel good about yourself and be proud of who you are and what you've done, it's not good to get a big head. Like it or not, there's always someone better than you. Obviously, nobody likes to hear this, but it's definitely the reality and couldn't be truer. The key is to stay humble and kind towards others even if they aren't as skilled as you in a certain area. Without being humble, success suddenly becomes more of a fantasy than a reality.

After you realize that you're just another drop in the ocean, you will greatly increase the likelihood of realizing your dreams. Success always starts with you first. Then, people will have an influence on you as you go throughout life. Some will be a positive influence and others will not. Stay clear of the ones who constantly put you down as you will want to give up. Nobody likes downers let's face it...they're just no fun to talk to. It's pretty cut and dry, be with those who talk you up and not down.

The power of just one compliment is sometimes underestimated. People will act like it's a little thing but it's much more. Complimenting others will put you closer to success and further away from failure than you might think. Even if you're having a bad day and it just seems as if nothing can look up then it's probably not a bad idea to help someone else with their problems. It may sound strange, but once you help somebody with their issues then your problems seem to diminish. Not only is that a win for you, but that's a win-win situation altogether!

Problems are only as bad as you make them and your success is only as good as you make it. Don't focus on your errors unless you strive to fix them, but if you have no intention on fixing them then it's best to move on, realizing there's always another opportunity. Remember to not wait around for every potential opportunity though.

Usually, you'll need to go after what you want since opportunities typically don't come every day. Just keep getting out of bed knowing that you have a purpose and that you're nowhere near being a failure as long as you keep grinding.

Rule #3- Stay True to Yourself

It's sadly common for most people to want to be someone that they're not just to please others. Generally, this tactic will work for some time and will trick others into believing their fake persona, but it's almost always short-lived. It's necessary to avoid being just another artificial person in society unless you plan on being untrustworthy. Respectable people dig those who are real and completely down to earth. The more real you are, the more people will realize it.

No matter where you are, what the situation is...just stay true to yourself and please nobody but yourself. Make yourself happy and proud by being real. Don't succumb to peer pressure and hate. Don't do things others want you to do especially if it will make you unhappy. It's YOUR life and nobody else's.

Sticky situations will continue to arise in everybody's life and it gets really hard if your own family doesn't support your goals and expectations. They are probably the people you want to please most. Do your own thing even if your family doesn't want it that way. Usually, you can't have it both ways. Not every single situation will pan out the perfect way. You need to do what's best for you. Always fight through every problem like it's your last fight. Keep the dream alive and well regardless of outside circumstances. Simply be you and only you whether others like you or not.

You are very special regardless of what others think. Life is an incredible journey. Why would you bother going down the walk of life if you are not well...being you? Society is at least partially to blame for creating this desire to be fake. From chemically-enhanced food, to plastic

8

surgery and to yellow journalism, it's no surprise that we currently are living in an artificial world.

Furthermore, ours is a "microwave" culture. Everything always has to be brief and straight to the point. If not, people will get bored of the subject. In the grand scheme of things, don't let society shape who you are and how you will react. You must shape yourself. Letting society shape you is just as bad as if a parent were to let a kid teach them how to parent. Simply take charge of your life knowing that you can be you and that is all that truly matters.

Has somebody ever told you that your body is repulsive and that you should be ashamed of it? If so, the person is more than likely jealous of how you look. Now, everyone can and should continuously improve their physique. Your body is under constant construction but that doesn't mean that you need to be ashamed of how you presently look. Cherish what is important to you. Everybody treasures something different from the next person. Don't let anybody steal your treasure. If you're proud of how you look, then you're welcome to stay looking that way if you wish. It's a part of you that keeps you hopeful.

Understand that nobody can attain the "perfect body" but you can always improve it. Always remember to learn as you go, but most importantly...don't forget to enjoy the ride. Time goes by much too quickly for you to not enjoy the life you have been given. Ultimately, do what makes you, you, so you don't have to worry about having regrets. You can count on being unhappy if you live your life behind a mask. It's better to make yourself happy and disappointing certain people versus making yourself unhappy to please others. You have to be true to yourself before you can ever begin to experience the joys of life. It's a pure tragedy to live a false life rather than a real one.

Rule #4: Break Your Long-Term Goals into Smaller Goals

Has it ever seemed like your ultimate goals are taking unbearably long? Well, most people have felt the same exact way. It's grueling trying to match all of your expectations while dealing with so many setbacks. Fortunately, there's an option to better deal with reaching your objectives. It may sound totally pointless, but compartmentalizing and handling piecemeal all those enormous targets you have set will dramatically decrease the hassle of trying to achieve it all at once. You may want to ask yourself a serious question. Would you want to eat breakfast, lunch, and dinner in one whole meal or would you prefer to wait and have three separate meals? The answer is obvious.

The glory of breaking your final goal into several smaller pieces will help you stay on track more efficiently. While you may very well be overwhelmed by the numerous parts of your objective, you still will feel much more assured in the long run knowing that you can focus on one tiny goal at a time. Cramming your dreams or anything else in for that matter has always had its disadvantages. It's never worked in our society yet and never will. By not cramming everything together, you will not only save yourself the headaches, but also the time that you would have had to commit to one big goal.

You may be wondering how much you should break each goal down. That greatly depends on how big that particular goal is in the first place. For example, let's say that you want to become the next top model. Well, there's a whole lot that goes into that one complex goal. While you're at it, it's good to note that being as detailed as possible is absolutely key in becoming triumphant. So instead of just hoping to be the next top model, you could say that you want to be the next top fitness model in the next couple of years. Or maybe you want to become the next top fashion model. It truly depends on the vision that you have laid out for yourself. Assuming that you have a strong desire to be the next top fitness model in the few years, you would need to get serious by making a point of toning up your body. Then from there it would be wise to get a gym membership, then simplify it from there by cutting out any unhealthy foods in your diet, and so on and so forth.

It sounds simple and of course it's easier said than done, but don't let that stop you! And if becoming the next top model isn't in your plans, then maybe opening up your own business is. This is yet another complicated goal, but not impossible! Again, this one will need to be simplified like any other major objective.

The first step to simplifying this goal would be to map out any future costs of resources and tools needed for your upcoming business. Next, would be to get business training so you know how to operate a business properly. And then, it would be wise to map out the best location for it sales wise but also make sure that your chosen location isn't going to violate any city laws! From there, it's smart to finance your business with loans, grants, etc. Afterwards, setting up the legal structure for your company is also key. You would need to decide which kind of ownership is right for you. Partnership, corporation, LLC, nonprofit, etc. Following that, registering it with your state government is critical! With this you'll be able to piece together which Tax ID number you'll need to receive from the IRS and your state revenue agency. And while these are the beginning stages of opening a business, there's much more that goes into it. It's an incredibly long process that can make you pant like a dog, but it can pay off for something amazing!

The work you put in for any specified goal may seem pointless and even in some cases counterproductive, but it is ultimately necessary. If you're serious about attaining something that is off-the-charts, then it's very important to take your mission seriously and to break that titanic goal into a bunch of smaller objectives! They say that if you can't run, then walk. And if you can't walk, then crawl. Never give up at any cost and always find ways to break your goals down into smaller bits. Even if your goal is pretty small to begin with, you still could break it into even smaller pieces yet so it's even manageable. It's just that simple! Yes, you heard right! The concept is extremely simple, but the work you have to put in and all the grinding you must do is a whole different ball game. Are you ready to grind? Are you ready to simplify your enormous goals into smaller ones so those huge dreams are easier to achieve?

Rule #5: Don't Strive for Perfection

Countless people endlessly pursue the route to perfection because they're afraid of failing. While you should strive to be the best that you can be, you shouldn't get all wrapped up in trying to be Mister Perfect. Perfection is literally unattainable no matter how hard and how much you try to achieve it. It's nothing more than a fantasy! This may sound entirely pessimistic, however, it's totally different from that. It may not be an optimistic viewpoint either, but it's a completely realistic one. The main reason why one should never ever attempt to be perfect is because they'll inevitably disappoint themselves. Learn to be more content in your life. This may sound simple and unworthy of trying, but without any kind of contentment in one's life you'll be totally unhappy each and every day. Now you may think if you're content, then you have to accept your life as it is and that you shouldn't strive for anything more or less. That's not entirely true, while you should be satisfied with your life, you should still have a will to want to always improve. Basically, be content with the positive, but constantly have a strong will to alter your lifestyle habits for the better. Keep in mind that it's not always going to be a cakewalk! The race is oftentimes very long and tiring, but take heart though in knowing that you can overcome any obstacle and dash to the finish line.

You may also feel as if many of the people, specifically, the celebrities on television are 'living the dream', or in other words, may have the 'perfect' life. Well, the media has a really funny way of making their lives seem glamorous 24/7, although, it's not always quite like that. Their life is certainly easier than the average person's, but their life also comes with struggles just like anybody else's. Life is full of disappointments for everyone. You are guaranteed to face difficulties no matter how rich or poor. So, don't ever let the media brainwash you into believing otherwise. The media gives a false perception on celebrities and their lifestyles. NOBODY'S life is perfect.

Other people who may not even be deep in fame and fortune may still come up to you and bragging about how amazing their life is, but it's usually somewhat tempered. Typically, that's their way of coping with the issues in their life as it helps make them feel better. It's basically a way for them to create a 'fantasy reality' where everything is always going well one hundred percent of the time. Don't fall for these lies that people tell you about their lives. Understand that your life can be just as good as anybody else's but always realize it won't be perfect either. If all else fails and you still find yourself struggling to be fully content with your life, then you must remember that you should avoid chasing the wind at all as you will never catch it and instead will always be left disappointed.

Rule #6: Don't Underestimate the Power of You

You are you, that is what's so neat. Just the simple fact that you were born is truly a miracle much more than words can even describe! You can do anything that you want to do! They say that life is only ten percent of what happens to you and the other ninety percent is how you respond. If this quote contained any more truth it would flood every lie that exists today! The idea is insanely easy: don't let others affect how you feel about every situation in your life because once you let them hinder your mood, then your entire day will gradually become a gigantic mess of negativity. The law of attraction is very real as you get back what you put out. Don't be weak and submit to everyone else's opinions and feelings. You and ONLY you have control of your actions and how you respond.

Do you think that you are utterly powerless? Do you think that everybody has dominion over you? Well, do yourself a huge favor and delete those thoughts. The sooner the better!

The only opinion that should ever matter throughout your whole entire life should be yours. You can either set yourself up for inevitable failure or inevitable success. Which would you rather have? Basically, anyone would always take success over failure especially if it's inevitable. Now, there are countless things in life that we honestly have no control over at all. For instance, you cannot control and choose who your parents and siblings will be or when you're born. However, most things in this world are controllable. Essentially, you are exactly what happens to you.

Since you know that you are the controller of your life and that you practically control most of your outcomes, then your way to success is much clearer. Go out and prove to your haters that you are capable of what you speak. Don't even back down for a second! Don't roll over in submission! You can achieve what you desire, but just don't tire. The very worst possible thing that you could do to yourself and to your reputation is if you would fold. If you were playing cards would you just fold and walk out the door in anger? Maybe. If you don't have the drive to keep going that is. Don't spend your time around unsupportive people. Ever! All they will do is wear your drive out and then your drive will die once you fully allow them to kill it. Take charge of what you want. Defend what you want before you even attain it. Your goals have your name stamped on them and nobody can take that away from you but yourself. You are so powerful that you can either choose to win or lose. You have the ultimate choice on whether you will live or die. You have the decision on whether you would prefer to have hope or have fear. This is how amazingly powerful you are as a being. It may sound naive but your destiny undoubtedly depends on your choices and their outcomes. Your choices always determine the good or bad of how things turn out. Of course, you can always have somebody else try and make all of your decisions; but what will that ever do for you? You need to make choices, specifically good well-thought out ones, and learn as you go. Even though you will make mistakes it's alright. Simply look at them and realize that you won't make the same mistakes again. The worst mistakes are the ones that you keep making and not the ones that you only have made once before.

Be thankful for all the good that has come to you. Be positive in knowing that the best is yet to come. Stay hopeful when fear seems to be gripping hold of your life. Remain calm and know that you can and will be in control. The law of attraction is very powerful. It may sound like nothing but a silly theory that probably holds no truth and is total bogus, but it surprisingly plays a big role in people's lives. What many fail to realize is that the more negative and discontent you are with your life, the longer that negativity will prevail. While the natural human reaction to negative situations is to get angry, you should refrain from as best you can or at least limit how angry you get. There's a very important reason why. Not only is it unhealthy to stay angry and keep getting mad, but anytime you have negative feelings it attracts negative circumstances. So how do you attract positive situations? It's fairly simple, well it's super simple actually. All you really need to do is be positive and, thus, you will be attracting positive results. Along with attracting these confident results, will come positive people. So, if you're seeking in a positive light, people then always remember to remain optimistic. Again, you are your own master! Never be tricked into believing that you have to be reliant upon somebody else when it comes to trying to complete day to day tasks. You control which flow you want in your life whether that's positive or negative.

Rule #7: Treat Luxuries like Your Necessities

We all crave new things and it seems like the list of our desires simply never ends. While it's certainly a good idea to be content, you also should realize that striving for new and better things isn't bad either. Needs are obviously more important than wants, have always been, and always will be, however, there's a specific power in treating your everyday wants like your everyday needs. Have you ever seemed to notice that when one person desperately needs something they'll do almost anything in their power to get it? For example, if a homeless person is chomping at the bit to get even a small burger they will fight for it until they can satisfy their hunger. Well, if you fought to get your wants like a homeless person fights for food and water, then you would find that the struggle wouldn't be so immense.

Let's say that you want a brand-new game system or even better yet a Rolls Royce. The bigger the luxury the better, but it seems unattainable, doesn't it? The possibility of getting what you want always seems to be slim to none when you hear the cost. No price tag and no roadblock should stop you and limit to what you want to get or do with your life. Even though price tags do unfortunately play a huge role in people's everyday lives, we can always overcome what we are limited to buy. The idea of the solution is simple, get a better income, but the work required to up your annual income isn't so simple. This should not stop you either. Try new things that you love and start it off as a hobby. Grind endlessly at what you're wanting to achieve like your life depends on it. Roadblocks are always bound to be ahead of you and your dreams, but if you're sincere and passionate then you have no choice but to fight for it. You will have to face your fears, step out of your comfort zone, and face other obstacles.

A great way to attain something that may be temporarily out of our budget is to save up money. You should do this religiously for best results. Yes, it sounds like a terrific idea, but when you apply it, it's so much harder to do. Temptations are always surrounding us to buy this, buy that, and everything that you lay your eyes on. You should absolutely buy what you want now and then to treat yourself, just like you should occasionally have a cheat day when eating on a healthy meal plan, but always remember to stay focused and not overspend.

When you need food and water you must put that at the top of your list since they are needs, right? Well, when you want something so badly and don't have the money at the moment to purchase it, then you should conserve the few extra dollars you have over the period of months and sometimes even years. The more money saved, the closer you are to buying that next special luxury. The point is, treat your wants with as much priority as you do with your needs.

Have you ever been so incredibly hungry that you would literally eat just about anything? Well, several people have been victims of this scenario, but maybe if you would have the same hunger for your desires then you wouldn't "underfeed" yourself and fall short of your goals each time. When you do something halfway right or worse yet, if you purposely try to do a task halfway correct, then not only are you underfeeding yourself, but you are prolonging the path to your dreams. You probably will never get to where you want to be unless you take it seriously. The reality is a blunt one, yet, it is a reality that should be noted. Yes, literally noted and even embedded in your mind. You can't expect for a minute that you will be successful if you don't first take the initiative. Everything always starts with you in the beginning. You had a beginning and so do your goals. Besides, you always are improving when you grow up so why can't you always continue progressing at your goals as well? There's simply no excuse to justify why you would sit down and stop working fiercely at your objectives. If you decide to sit down and wait for everything to work out for you then you will be utterly disappointed. It's not what people really want to hear. Most people want to be rich and famous, yet, most don't want to grind their way there. You always need to work for what you love, unless of course you are born into a wealthy family. Unfortunately, most of us fall in the category of the 'working-class' in this society, yet at the same time you will feel a better sense of accomplishment when you do achieve your dreams in comparison to the few who have been born rich. The reason for this is because many don't feel like they really did anything to get what they got and truthfully, when you're born into a rich family, you really didn't have to do anything. By the end of the day, you have no choice but to deal with the cards that you have been dealt and to make the best of it all. You will surely stumble and even fall, but if you keep the dream alive and keep going then you will never actually fail. It can't be stressed enough, act like getting your next luxury or desire is like getting your next meal.

Rule #8: Learn to Listen, Listen to Learn

You were born with two mouths and one ear, right? Wrong. Actually, we were all born bearing one mouth and two ears for a reason. As humans, we were and still are meant to listen more often than we speak. Speaking is without a doubt good when the time is right, but the more you listen then the more you will learn. Learning is a critical piece when you are striving to accomplish great things. The problem is many don't focus on learning and therefore don't take it seriously.

Many would rather procrastinate and watch Netflix or sit on social media scrolling through other people's feeds. If more people would take learning seriously and wouldn't stay wrapped up in their own world, then this world would be a much more advanced place. The idea is not rocket science. Use your ears more often than your mouth because there's always something to learn in this world.

Nobody knows everything ever. In life just when it seems like you have everything sorted and figured out, there's a curveball that comes by to test your knowledge and can sometimes even be a humbling experience.

Just imagine how much knowledge there still is yet to take in. The universe has infinite possibilities to it and there's no telling how much more each one of us can learn in our daily lives. A super important principle to keep in mind is to stay humble. Always, in every situation, stay humble. You will find that more doors will open up for you when you begin to humble yourself. Aside from just being humble, it's absolutely key to remain kind to others as you would expect them to be to you. Remember when you were a child and you were told to not speak unless spoken to? Well, there's a whole lot of truth in that. Of course, it's not bad to have nice, even lengthy conversations with others, but if you don't ever hear anybody out not only will you learn less in life, but you will also be less tolerated by your peers. So, let's say you wanted a possibility of getting a job. If you kept interrupting them in the interview, then that wouldn't go over too well and your chances of getting hired would more than likely crash to rock bottom. If you want to become a more knowledgeable person and a more liked person, then never ever interrupt a peer. It's really not a hard idea to grasp. While knowledge will lead you closer and closer to what you want, it's not the full thing. Knowledge is power, but without connections your knowledge will only go so far. You may have heard of the saying: "it's not about what you know, but who you know." Well, this saying is one of the realist sayings out there especially when it comes to success and the lust for it. You should crave important people just as much as knowledge to skyrocket you further towards your objectives.

The benefits simply go on and on when you choose to listen more than you speak. Actually, the benefits are endless. Not only is knowledge power, but if you decide to take time to listen to others then you don't have to worry about regretting anything. They say that you just might regret certain things that you say and that you would like to take back but when it comes to listening there isn't anything you would need to take back because you would only be hearing what others say. You're playing it safer and smarter when you choose to be the listener. Abraham Lincoln once said, "Better to remain silent and be thought a fool than to speak out and remove all doubt." Now that doesn't mean you should never speak at all, but it just means that you should think before you speak. Always remember to think long and hard in advance. Additional benefits of listening more often include: gaining more inside information, letting others know you care when you listen to them, etc.

Let's say that you want to get deeply involved in the acting profession and that you don't have much experience or exposure, well, you could look for some fantastic connections to help sneak you in the industry quicker. You wouldn't want to rush it, but you want to get in quickly. Well, it all comes back to listening once again. It may sound completely useless and foolish, but listening is of major help when it comes to trying to get successful in any industry. Of course, you want to talk to people of high status, but you want to take the time to listen to them thoroughly so you get very detailed information that can be very helpful to you in your aspiring career. There's a connection in every career that you can seek and find. Where you are located will, without a doubt, determine how many major connections you have near you. Even if you are in a rural location and can't seem to find any important looking people, then it wouldn't be a bad idea to relocate to Los Angeles or New York, especially if you're serious about the entertainment industry. Many people will tell you that and it's a good idea to listen and take what you want seriously.

Everybody started somewhere. Most start at the bottom and very few start at the top. Most people aren't even first-generation rich and it may sound unbelievable but most rich people today weren't born rich either. They usually build their wealth from lower levels through many different strategies. Listening to more polished and experienced people is what got many successful people to where they currently are today. So, what better time to use your ears more often than now?

Rule #9: Understand That Happiness Is a Journey

Oftentimes, many of us get wrapped up in believing that happiness only occurs when we have reached our destination. It does certainly feel nice when you finally arrive, but if you don't enjoy the ride then your destination won't feel as rewarding. It's entirely true that the journey isn't always a blast and it can get irritating waiting for things to come together, yet, there are a lot of pocket moments along the journey that can be very fun and enjoyable. It is key to not miss out on enjoying the small things throughout your life. Ups and downs are bound to happen in everybody's life regardless of financial status, gender, race, etc. Nobody is exempt from problems or solutions. The more you enjoy your life and focus on the present, the greater your future can and will become.

There's no doubt that so many of us are very impatient to see the final results. They say that Rome wasn't built in a day and that could not be said any better. If everything was handed to us from the beginning, then none of us would even feel any sense of accomplishment. Patience is one of the major keys to success and without patience this world wouldn't have advanced as much as it did. Everything is a process whether we want to accept it or not. The more restless you get, the longer everything will seem to take. It won't just seem like it's taking longer for you to reach your goals, but it will actually take longer. There are numerous reasons for this. For one, the more impatient you are the less positive you will end up being. This will inevitably cause negative energy to flow right out of you and into other people's daily lives. Surely you wouldn't want that to take place. The more negative energy you dish out, the more negative you will get back. This is all part of the law of attraction. If you seriously crave help from others and crave positive things to come into your life and other people's lives, then it's a novel idea to remain positive even under extremely horrible circumstances. Take one day at a time and take each day to put on a good, genuine smile. Journey on to happiness, one day at a time. Never lose your positivity.

Have you ever got lost on a hiking trip when you were really young? When you found your way out, did it ever seem like there was a huge feeling of joy? Well, this joyful feeling usually occurs in life when you seek something hard enough and then you find it. Basically, while the journey to success is typically a thorn in your side, it is a blessing in the long run. You are able to appreciate the calm more when you go through a bunch of storms. Let's just say that if you were to get a trophy right away instead of getting it for winning a soccer match. Wouldn't it feel much less rewarding? It would feel incredibly empty and awkward. It's totally nice to get things without having to work for them, but it's not usually realistic nor is it a good mindset to have. You will undeniably be happier if you take the journey and make a few mistakes along the way.

There has been a good few influential famous people who are in wealth up to their eyeballs and were handed that wealth when they were born. Without a surprise, they turned out to not feel accomplished. Some of the people in the Royal Family have been victims of this. They didn't need to do anything from the start, but they wish they would have had to. It may sound weird, but many people who are born into wealth wish they could have built their own wealth rather than just accepting that they are first generation rich. Never ever underestimate how powerful the journey will be in your life. In the long run, your journey is always of value and helps build your joy. You can let your journey either make you or break you. Whether the adventure to your dreams is hard or not, you can't collapse and let go of all of your positivity. Your joy and your struggle can and will always trump any amount of hate and problems. Do yourself a huge favor and do not get down. Just because you may be down on your luck does not mean that you have to be down yourself. The quicker you realize that problems are always bound to occur, the quicker you can prepare yourself for them so you can overcome them much easier. It would be great if we lived in a utopian society where nothing could ever go wrong, yet, this just will never be reality. Sadly, every one of us live in a harsh reality full of problems, but with problems come solutions.

Along the journey to success many will mess up. It's good to stay happy with yourself and love yourself even when you succeed and even when you slip up. You can't be so hard on yourself because if you are always hard on yourself, then you will constantly disappoint yourself. You will get disappointed a whole lot on this long, drawn-out hike towards your aspirations and disappointments are impossible to avoid, yet, you can limit how many you get.

Staying negative or pessimistic will bring more disappointments your way. It's a self-fulfilling prophecy. You can choose to be positive and attract more positive results than negative results, or you can do it the other, less preferred way. Again, you are in absolute control of how you wish to respond to many of the curveballs that life throws at you. You see, it's not necessarily what's pitched to you, but how you strike it. You can either maintain your positive energy, enjoy your journey towards your dreams, and run the home run or you can allow yourself to get three strikes.

There are dozens of triumphant people in society who regret taking advantage of simply enjoying the ride. Many of them forgot how important it was to take even a few moments just to stop and smell the roses. It will seem like a huge time waster and very meaningless, but it's much more than you think.

Typically, you don't know what you have until it's gone. So many people will prolong doing things until the last minute or they will just not do it at all and regret it. Sometimes the little things become the biggest things in the long run of this whole journey. If it's going to be a long journey, then you may as well make it a good one. So, while you keep racing after what you want, make sure to just take a few breaks now and then to look outside at the incredibly beautiful nature that surrounds us all. After that you can once again smile and then grind your way up to the top and never ever stop!

Rule #10: Treat Your Dreams like a Spouse

When the bridge on your path seems uneven and crooked, walk on it. When the bridge on your path is shaky, prowl over it. When the bridge on your path is destroyed, jump over it. Don't let anybody divorce you from your dreams. Through your journey you will need to remain joyful and cheat on your fears. Would you let anybody ever steal the women or man of your dreams? It would be a tragedy to let your true love be taken away for good. The right one is there somewhere for you and your destiny in your goals are too. In fact, your future spouse goes hand in hand with your dreams! After all, they are basically your dream, right? The dream of you having them in your possession is very important (obviously more important than your other goals). At the same time, you don't want to go off on a tangent where you neglect pursuing your dreams and only focus on looking for girls. It is very important to search for dates and even though having the love of your life is a top priority, you should put it temporarily on the back burner while you still strive for your goals. They say that if you focus on your goals first, then the women will follow later. So, ultimately, if you do treat your goals like a spouse you will not only drastically increase your odds for success, but you will also end up with a spouse.

You can have a passion for basically anything and everything in this entire universe, but it all comes down to how passionate you are about it. Once you find what you are madly in love with, you need to seek it to the point of exhaustion. Success is never an easy nor a free ride. It never ever has come easy, still hasn't and never will. Stay in the fight and even when you are knocked down on your knees or even flat on your back, you still can't quit. It's not over until it's over! It may even sound weird, but grow an attraction towards what you've been wanting for all this time. Not necessarily a physical attraction, but a mental attraction. You need to be mentally strong just as you would need to be in any given relationship. Armor yourself up as if you were going to war with all of your troubles in your life. You cannot ever be defeated in this long battle for a bright future. Never grow tired of seeking your plan, fighting for it, and repeating the process all over again. Just like with a girl, it may seem like you rarely get anywhere when you try to communicate with her, perhaps because she's quiet or even in some cases very rude. Everything can get repetitive especially if you continue to put up with it, yet, sometimes you need to get at least somewhat redundant in your lifelong journey for your aspiration as you may need to repeat some actions again and again.

For example, if you wanted to be an actor you would need to look over your lines a good couple of times every day so you can memorize it efficiently and effectively. It may get grueling working endlessly and constantly at what you want in a repetitive manner, yet, you can never fold on what you have been longing for. You have to stay madly in love with the desires that, well, make you, you.

It's never truly possible to be happy when you're always doing what you hate the most. Likewise, it's basically impossible to be angry when you are doing what you've been always wanting to do. Realistically, there are still happy moments even if your career isn't what you like and there are also sad moments even if you're doing what you really love. All in all, if you don't do what you love then you will find yourself being unhappy more times than not. You would not ever want to be dating someone that you are unhappy with. It would be a miserable act to stay committed to one who is always bringing you down with them. It is the same idea with your career. You can't allow yourself to be brought down time and time again. Don't surrender yourself to what you despise. Don't ever roll over in submission! It's much easier to do so rather than fully achieving your plans, yet, it's far from wise. It's the exact opposite of wisdom.

Don't ever be afraid to fully let loose and take in the desires that you have for your future. Never be scared to express how passionate you are about your future endeavors. Many people will underestimate the love you have for your passion and several will even think you're foolish and that you don't have what it takes to make it. All you need to do is completely shut them out for good and realize they're jealous and have hopes of making you fail just like them. Certain people will even tell you that you can't get really attractive girls, yet, you can't let that discourage you. Do you think, out of the many pretty girls out there, that they will tell you no just because of what some people may try to embed in your mind? In the end, they will realize that looks aren't all of it. The initial attraction is awesome, but in the end, it's mainly your personality that's key. Who cares what others say about your looks or if they claim that you don't have the ability to make anything of yourself. You are as attractive as you choose to be and you are as able to grab hold of your dreams as anyone else. All it comes down to is you needing to have the drive or hunger to want to work harder towards your plans. Treat your goals like a spouse--with care! Don't quit on your dreams just like you wouldn't on your spouse. Cheat on your fears. Break up with your doubts. Get engaged to your faith and marry your dreams.

As long as you are determined to do well, there's nothing that can ever come between and your dreams.

Rule #11: Find and Fulfill Your Purpose

Have you ever been around a downtown area of a major city at night and seen a bunch of homeless people just scattered around trying to sleep? It seems as if there is no hope for them whatsoever and that their purpose in life is completely neglected. Or in other cases you may have people in steady jobs where they are making a decent income, but they just can't get into what they are doing. Whether you're rich, poor, or middle class if you are not fulfilling your purpose then you will never be truly happy. Without your purpose you are empty and there's a huge void. You can't let this void appear in your life because once it does it will take over your emotions and you will find it very difficult to be genuinely happy again. Whatever it is that you may get into, you need to find it and that comes with trial and error. You will need to try a lot of different hobbies that you like but you will more than likely fail many times before finding what you really are interested in. Don't let that discourage you because after banging your head against the wall enough, you will finally find what feels right. Murphy's law claims that if anything can go wrong, it will. While this is unfortunately a truth, there is also a better and more positive way of looking at life. For instance, if anything can go right, it will go right. Good can happen just as much as bad can but it's your choice if you want to look at the glass half-empty or half-full. Most of life is in your control and nobody else's. That is the glory of it!

Once you finally find what seems to be your obsession you will see your life start to advance before your very eyes. You will realize that even though it took a bit of time to find your passion, it was well worth the wait. Never forget that good things always come to those who wait. Many people who are finally successful and that have accomplished wonderful things have worked endlessly. After you do find your obsession you can't stop there and take a breath. You will need to remain patient but also hard working to ensure that you can get the job done. Besides, what better fulfillment is there than to work hard for your ultimate purpose.

If it seems that finding your purpose is the most challenging thing to do in the whole wide world, then it wouldn't be a bad idea to talk to a loved one to get any additional help with finding yourself. You will always find that you have plenty of options for how you wish to live your life now and for years to come. You can either head down the path that seems to be a wonderful but is instead toxic for your life or you can decide to go down the path that may not seem as glamorous, but turns out to be the better of the two. Usually it's wise to take the road less traveled. This is the case for countless reasons with one being that if you are a follower and always follow the crowd you may end up in really sticky situations. The last thing you would ever want and need is to be stuck in a hole that you can't dig yourself out of. If you follow the wrong crowd and can't ever have good judgement, then you'll be fogging the road towards finding and fulfilling your purpose in life.

It may seem like a mystery on who you should hang around with when so many people are substance abusers. Believe it or not, there are still many good people out there who are a good influence to others. If you choose to surround yourself with peers who are not always getting drunk and high then you will not only have better people to hang around with, but then you will also have more support in finding your real and true purpose in this confusing world. Nothing was ever meant to be easy in this life for anyone, but if you at least spend time with the right people who have the right morals and values then your life and future will be laid out so much simpler.

Aside from trying out several different hobbies and hanging out with the right people, you also want to consider traveling a great deal. Travel is the only thing you buy that makes you come out richer. The wonderful thing about traveling from place to place is that you see fresh, brand new experiences everywhere you to go. It's a spark that you add to your life that hardly is there unless something new comes up. It's a good kind of spark though. It helps expand your mind and, in turn, your horizons. Traveling tends to be neglected by so many. It's not always treated as something important in people's daily lives. Some even go as far as to say that traveling isn't exactly necessary, but this couldn't be farther from the truth. When you vacation, you automatically are enlightened. Just when you take a few steps outside the door, you are already on the path to enlightenment.

Never take traveling, close family and friends, or any second of your life for granted.

Make every single second count to you because your life counts in your family's eyes. Just because you don't see your purpose right now doesn't mean that you won't ever see it and attain it. Every purpose is worth searching for and fulfilling and yours is too! Be patient and know that you will ultimately be pleased beyond your wildest dreams when you find what you have been looking for. Don't worry about what you're looking for since you will find what you're looking for.

Rule #12: Take Action...NOW!!

Action is one of the most powerful acts you can do. When somebody talks and talks about something they really want badly they usually go off on a tangent and never stop speaking out about it. Words are also pretty powerful but nothing can compare with taking action. Taking the proper and necessary action is huge! Nothing can match it. Actions always speak louder than words. It may seem like just because someone decides to say something that they may mean it but sadly that isn't always the case. There's a saying: you can talk the talk but some can't walk the walk. You may have dealt with a whole bunch of people who would overpromise and instead underdeliver. That's disappointing. Unfortunately, you can't control what other people will promise you and how they may deliver, but you can at least control yourself on that issue. Only promise what you know you can deliver. You can set yourself apart from so many others that way. Sometimes it may even be better to not say what you want to do and just do it instead. Wouldn't you rather just do what you've been wanting instead of just talking about it? All talk and no action is a killer for success and happiness and will keep you stagnant or it may even make your life situations worse. Let's face it, a stagnant life is a boring life. You're procrastinating when you continue to be a talker instead of a doer. Doers are much more victorious and happy versus talkers and they always will be. There's no better feeling than doing something and seeing the results unfold before you. You will have a very strong sense of pride when you finally stand up and take charge for your future.

When it comes to chasing fiercely after what we want, we occasionally face periods where we may have to do what we hate in order to finally get to where we've always been wanting to be.

Let's say that you want to be a full-time model, but you still aren't completely there yet. While you may crave modeling as a career, you can't always just jump right in from the start. Unfortunately, you would at the very least need to get a part time job for cash flow while you still grind towards getting what you've always wanted. In life we need to take action not only for things we love, but in certain scenarios also for things we possibly hate. You definitely don't want to get caught up in doing things you are disgusted with, but sometimes there's a price that needs to be temporarily made. Sacrifices need to be made from time to time. Luckily, these sacrifices aren't going to last forever and good things are yet to come and even greater ones following that.

Making your move for what you're wanting is undoubtedly awesome, but there's more to it than that. It's not just about taking the proper action, but it's also about the timing. The older and wiser you get, the more you will begin to realize that timing is everything in even the smallest and easiest of circumstances. Even if you indeed are taking the correct action for what you want but aren't doing it at the right time, then you are blockading yourself from going one hundred percent or all out in other words. Aside from just timing, you want to understand that being in the right place is also critical in determining how far you will go on this journey. You may not have found the right place just yet to be in and you may not have found the perfect timing either but the key is to be patient. Always be patient even after you make your move for your passions. It seems like the many people who have made it all the way to the very top have got there overnight with not much of a delay at all. In all actuality, all of these people or at least most of them have been stuck waiting almost endlessly to accomplish their dreams. The road to success is never clear. It's practically a road that has bumps on every part of it along with a whole bunch of fog surrounding it. Keep in mind though that just because you should be patient on this tiresome journey, you still should keep the grind going no matter what.

Patience doesn't mean you should just lie back and expect everything to simply come together like puzzle pieces for a puzzle, but it means that you should keep working hard while still waiting on the results.

You may feel lost and confused constantly and you may not know who you are as a person, but in the grand scheme of things, your actions are what defines you as a person and nothing else. Who you are isn't based upon your looks, age, or the color of your skin but upon you are as a person inside. You don't ever need to question who you are to people. Even if you, yourself, don't know yourself who you are, all it takes is to keep trying new things and putting yourself out there.

There might be numerous factors out there that keep you from following the steps to get to where you want to be. One could very well be fear and this is probably the main one. Fear can be just as deadly as procrastination as they both can hinder you from fully dedicating yourself to your goals. Fear is the only thing to fear. That's how truly powerless fear is! It is only as powerful as you allow it to be. No amount of fear can harm you. As long as you stay focused and determined on what you believe is yours then nothing or nobody can or will ever stop you. As soon as you take action and stop procrastinating, the quicker you will begin to see your destination off in the distance. The longer you stay committed to these goals, the closer you will be to finally greeting your destiny.

Rule #13: Be Motivated by the Fear of Being Average

Do you ever get a bad feeling inside that you may just turn out to be yet another average person? Sadly, many usually go through this phase and don't always see a way out of this lousy feeling right away. Being average is undeniably a huge quality that our society accepts. If anything, we should frown upon it heavily and even dismiss the idea completely. It may be the preferred path to take for your future as being mediocre is definitely not a very difficult road, yet in the long run you may very well be disappointed by the choices you made.

Fear is often frowned upon. It's a quality you don't want to have otherwise others will look at you like you are a total wimp. It certainly will hinder you from releasing your full potential, but it isn't always a negative characteristic to have. If you use your fears to motivate yourself then they automatically start affecting you and your future life in a positive manner. You basically are using negative energy and transferring it to positive energy and then using that positive energy to better your life. When you allow your fears to motivate you to be better than the average Joe, you then set yourself apart from everybody else.

Every person who gained success in singing, acting, modeling, bodybuilding, and so on has had the fear of being average at least once. Once they got the fear built up in them, they looked at their present life, stood up, and then declared that a huge change will need to be made in their lives in order for them to reach their goal. It doesn't matter if your goal happens to be big or small. What truly matters is how motivated you choose to be in order to finally attain it. You can let your dreams be dreams every day you wake up, but that won't cut it. The closest you will ever get to living your dreams is in your dreams unless you fully decide to take control of what you really want.

Sometimes it will take staying up a little later than usual just to get a few extra things done. That's what the price comes out to be especially when you are running away from mediocrity. You can either choose to live your dreams in your sleep or you can pick losing a little extra sleep and ultimately begin to live your dreams when you're awake. It's as simple as that.

Motivation is the key to success. Without this key you can count on never being able to unlock the door of your dreams. What good is it to just lay around and procrastinates all day? You will never get a single thing done without motivation. And the right motivation. Without the proper inspiration, you surely will feel like giving up very quickly.

Sometimes it takes looking at other people's lives to get yourself fully motivated. People are always influencing others in many ways in a positive or negative way. You can bet that you will be influenced by someone along the way if you search hard enough. The key is to find someone who was struggling in their life, but then gradually overcame their problems. Once you can find that someone, you could very well be influenced in a good way and then they could be your inspiration for life. People are not always capable of giving themselves the correct type and amount of motivation. Sometimes it's necessary to look at someone's life story of how they were able to become victorious in order to get the inspiration you've been needing all along.

A person can be average in many different aspects of their life. It isn't always career-based, they can also be average in their personality with how they treat others. Someone could even be above average in a certain area of their life and average in another. For example, one could have an above average physique, but a very mediocre personality. Let's say you were someone who had a bad personality and weren't really liked. You likely wouldn't have very many friends and would be fairly lonely. That right there would bring great fear to you if you were in that scenario. The problem that many face is that they aren't humble enough to accept the fact that they have fears. Everybody has things that will frighten them. Some people have more terror than others, but nobody is exempt. The black hole that you must avoid at all costs is being arrogant enough to the point where you can't accept the fact that you are human and have fears like every other person. When you become arrogant, you start plateauing. This is when you start becoming very unsuccessful.

In order to eventually become triumphant, you must remain humble by understanding that you do in fact have fears. Once you can acknowledge that, you can then start using your fears for your own good. Without fears, nobody would be anywhere. You need a little fear in your life. Fear is usually a missing ingredient in the recipe for success as many don't allow themselves to get scared enough to do better than the bare minimum. Our world would not be as advanced as it currently is without people having the fear of losing something in their lives. Businessmen who nearly have had their businesses shut down worked extra hard to keep it running as they feared losing their businesses completely, soldiers work extra hard to protect their country as they have a fear of it being taken over, and so on. These are just a couple examples of how much harder certain people tend to work than the average person because they allowed their fears to be evident and then they got motivated from them to do even better. If others can become motivated, you can too!

Rule #14: Burn Your Ship

When the going gets tough people tend to give up. Usually it's that they give up far too early as they have fear of failing. In other words, they basically retreat from the grind that they had for their dreams. Many become victim to this scenario, but fortunately there's a tactic you can use to prevent this from occurring in your life while you march on the road to success. It's a tactic known as 'burning your ship'. They say that if you want to conquer an island then you must first burn your ship. It may sound silly and counterproductive perhaps, but if you constantly leave yourself the option for retreat then you will surely retreat. However, if you decide to remove the choice of retreating from your life, then you are forced to grind no matter what is thrown your way. After all, the road to victory is always a long and hard one and you need the mindset that you can and will destroy any and every challenge that is thrown at you.

The idea of preventing yourself from retreating is not focused on well enough by the many communities in the world. It's in fact hardly ever talked about and is perhaps one of the most crucial strategies anybody could ever even think about using. 'Burning your ship' isn't just a good method for people with a lot of fear to use, but it's also a wonderful method for procrastinators to try out. If you happen to be a procrastinator who enjoys putting things off to the next day, then you will suddenly see a bright and positive change in your life as well as the ones around you when you start to 'burn your ship'. By avoiding retreat, you have nowhere to run or hide and you can only win as a result. You won't be able to say that there's a tomorrow to do this or that. You will ultimately force yourself to face your goals and challenges head-on.

The glory of not retreating when things get tough is practically infinite. There are so many benefits that go along with being brave and facing your problems. One benefit in particular happens to be that you will just become a much better person in the long run. You may look at yourself months or even years down the road and examine the greatness that flourished in you when you first got bold enough to finally stand up for what you believed was yours and made no plan for retreat.

Just another perk of not wanting to withdrawal is that you will become a leader rather than a follower. You will become truly independent and will not have to take orders from anyone in your life when you fight for what you believe is yours. With independence and with being a leader, you will instead be able to tell others what they should be doing and how they can improve in their lives so they too can eventually go on to be leaders. This is a win-win situation for you as you can feel the joy of independence and also the joy of helping others become leaders just like you. Remember though that none of this can take place unless you sum up the courage to 'burn your ship'. Nobody is stopping you, but you!

Rule #15: Pay It Forward

The world as we know it seems very dark and full of misfortune. It seems that oftentimes we are swimming in an ocean of inconsiderate people. Certain people are not always the most welcoming and friendly, but believe it or not there still are good people in this world. It seems like hate has completely overthrown love, but thankfully that isn't the case. Love still has a stronghold in this world and it may take longer to find real, genuine love but it's worth the search because once you find it it's something special. Even when all else seems to be failing and it seems like nobody is spreading positivity, there is still hope and that hope starts with you.

The only hope of our society improving is to lift others up so we all rise together. Once you lift somebody up from a negative situation, you also do the same for yourself. Many people seem to expect good things in return for themselves after they help someone out, but that's a naive way of going about it. Instead, it's much better to not expect anything in return after helping the person in need. Acts of kindness should never be conditional whatsoever. They should be done just out of the goodness of your heart. After you understand that acts of random kindness should be unconditional, it's good to note that you should let them know to avoid repaying you for your good deed and instead tell them to pass it on to the next person or pay it forward. This allows them to pass kindness further down the line so it will reach more people. After all, gifts are meant to be paid forward and not paid back. Paying it forward is a very powerful act that can and will forever impact the world in a positive way! There's nothing more rewarding in a day than to do a good deed for somebody and have them not understand how to repay you.

The concept of paying the good deed forward is incredibly simple to fully grasp, yet, many seem to fail at going through with the idea. It's much easier to just expect something in return from somebody after you do something nice for them, but that's how most people fall short in this world. Just because something is easier doesn't necessarily mean it is indeed better. What is convenient and what is truly right are two entirely different things. If we strongly urge this society of ours to advance farther in a civil manner, then we have absolutely no choice but to take matters into our own hands and face the issue at stake. We need to spread peace, love, and positivity! The idea is so undeniably effortless that even a toddler could wrap their mind around it. The problem isn't that the idea is hard to understand but that the problem got so big because so many people neglected the idea. It wouldn't have been as bad if we just ignored the idea in comparison to literally neglecting the whole idea. Of course, ignoring issues are about as bad, but neglecting something is a more aggressive way of ignoring something. This is generally how most problems occur and worsen. Neglect is the rejection of a positive and successful society. This may sound very cliché but we need to neglect the neglection. We can't keep neglecting this issue in our world any longer.

It all comes back down to taking the proper action. Situations will only continue to worsen at a rapid rate if we don't decide to finally put our foot down. If you want to be successful and you want to improve this world, then it would be wise to get out and start helping people in need. If you ever feel like you are having a horrible day of constant bad luck, then start helping others. If you are having an amazing day that is full of warmth and happiness, then help others. Basically, whether you are having a day of abundant joy or a day of abundant misfortune, never underestimate how uplifting it is to help another person out. After all, you may never know when you're in a sticky situation and you need somebody's help.

Happiness is always a journey and it's up to you if you want to make your journey an enjoyable one. It could be miserable or it could be outstanding, but either way you need to help out others to help out the world and in turn yourself as well. Even when you pay it forward and you don't get anything in return, you still kind of do believe it or not. The simple joy that radiates off them will transfer to you and will drown you in it and then you will become that joy. No single amount of money is better than the precious gift of joy. The only time that money will really give you real joy is when you buy someone something that they always needed but may never have had before. For instance, purchasing a bed for someone who never has had a bed for themselves is a special moment or perhaps you do something as simple as paying for the next person's groceries in the grocery store. When you begin to help others out especially in a consistent manner, then you will begin to see that your problems aren't as bad as you originally thought they were.

For the record, the more you assist other people and not just yourself, you will see that you will become more well-liked and respected in civilization. Happiness will also begin to seem limitless and problems will begin to seem limited. There will still be struggles along the way, but when you become a helpful part of society, then you will find life become much more bearable. Don't hesitate! Begin today! There's always someone needing help and all you have to do is be there. Make a difference. Every little help gradually becomes a big help over time. Make somebody smile today and then they can pass it along. Before you know it, the world will be in an endless loop of glowing positivity!

Rule #16: Don't Compare Yourself with Others

Comparing ourselves to others is a very common thing that many of us seem to do. If it were a disease, we all would likely be dead or at least so sick to the point where we would want to just fall back and die. There are a lot of 'relationship killers' that people tend to do to one another and some things people do to each other are worse than others, but nothing can compare with comparing. Literally.

Comparing is one of the worst things you could do with someone, if not the very worst. When you choose to compare with another person you are already setting up the relationship to fail miserably. Not to mention, you are causing yourself to become discontent. The more you compare, the more discontent you are destined to become in life.

It's one thing to see what you may have in common with another peer, but it's another to decide to go off on a tangent of pure, hardcore comparison. If you choose to constantly be competitive, you will find that more and more people begin to distance themselves from you. Unfortunately, some people lose friends and they don't ever seem to realize why. Now, certain friends aren't good to have and it's not a bad idea to cut them from your life, but it's good to occasionally take a look in the mirror just to keep yourself in check. There are toxic people but sometimes the toxic person could very well be you. That may not be the case necessarily, but it's good to glance over yourself and make sure you are treating others correctly.

Friends are the extra set of keys you need to unlock the doors in life that you can't unlock yourself. Ultimately, they can help slingshot you in anything you want to do. So, be careful how you treat them and keep check of how competitive you get. There's a fine line between competitive and ultra-competitive. For example, it's one thing to have fun playing a soccer game with friends, but it's another to not understand how to take a loss and to yell and argue with your peers over some petty game or contest.

You never know when you need the help of anyone, let alone your friends. Help can be needed whether you have huge aspirations or not. Perhaps you currently are a talented local rapper and want to get yourself out there more but you don't currently have the best of connections. Maybe you only know so many people that can only do so much which turns out to not be very much at all. You may think in that scenario that you don't have much more hope left, but let's say that your best friend has a cousin who is a talented rapper as well and is also touring several cities across America. Unfortunately, you fought with your best friend because you always tried to outdo him and you now don't talk anymore and you need him in order to get in touch with his cousin. If that were the real case scenario for you presently, then you would likely be very disappointed and even upset. You see, this is what happens in situations when you choose to outdo the next person even if it isn't your friend. Just comparing in general is deadly to anybody who does it and for the people who are victim to the comparison.

There's a time and place for everything and anything that you choose to do or say. Just like there is a time to sleep, eat, and exercise, there's also a time when you actually could compare and have the results turn out positive for once.

Compare is without a doubt viewed as a negative word and rarely viewed as a positive one. Competition has also been quite the friend to our society as competition has allowed it to advance rather quickly. Businesses in general have come a long way with the new technology. Where there is competition, there is either progression or digression. You may sometimes think that comparing is only good when it comes to companies that always rival each other, but that's not exactly the case. Comparing can be an awesome thing to do in your life when you do it the right way. If you choose to compare yourself in the here and now in comparison to your past self then that's absolutely splendid. There's really no better feeling than seeing how much and how well you improved from the old you from months or even years back to today.

Comparing can also be a very excellent decision to make when you may need to pick what lifestyle is right for you. Maybe you need to select between a lifestyle of smoking several packs of cigarettes and sitting on the couch or instead eat healthy, avoid tobacco, and exercise daily. It's pretty straightforward as comparisons aren't at all bad unless you allow them to be. It all comes down to how are you comparing and what are you comparing with. If you work out specifically with weights and want to compare your muscles now to how they looked back then, it wouldn't at all be a horrible idea to take progress pictures from how you looked months back to now. These progress pictures will be responsible for boosting your self-confidence and will give you a sense of satisfaction knowing that you are indeed making progress on your body. By the end of the day, as long as you are not always trying to outdo the person next door or your friends and family then you will notice yourself being happier with yourself as a whole. Contentment is always a wonderful thing to have even when you keep striving for more.

There's a rule that many of us don't ever seem to follow or at least not very well. This rule is known as the 'golden rule'. It claims that you should treat others how you would like to be treated. It's a pretty basic rule but still is an excellent rule to hold onto and follow. If someone were to compare themselves with you then chances are that you probably wouldn't appreciate it one single bit. In fact, you might even get a little upset. It would probably be the same way for them if you were to compare yourself right to them. In the grand scheme of things, everybody has their own skills as well as flaws and there's no reason to always wish to rival the next person who you face throughout your lifetime. Everybody is special in their own way and their specialties may seem quite minor to you, but that doesn't mean they're any worse than you and it also doesn't mean that you are any better than them either. Remember to stay civil to others as you wish they would to you also. Also, never forget that there's a fine line between pulling somebody's leg and actually comparing with them. Knowing all this will no doubt allow you to keep healthy and steady relationships with others as well as just being a more content person all around.

Rule #17: Ignore Criticism but Embrace Constructive Criticism

Throughout the course of your life there will always be a critic or hater who will attempt to knock you down whenever possible. You once again are able to control how you handle situations like this. Life will happen to you, but it's up to you how you decide to respond. Let's face it, nobody ever enjoys battling through difficult and heartbreaking areas in their life, but sometimes we have no choice but to go all in and confront the problems we have been ignoring. When you finally summon up the courage to go all in and face your issues, you will sometimes get knocked down. All you need to do then is get right back up. You really need to take note of this especially when it comes to harsh criticism from a person and even more so when it's heavy criticism from your friend or family member. They say that the ones we love do in fact hurt us the most. Usually, a friend or family member would be the last person to ever think about criticizing you, some still do.

It's key to understand the difference between regular criticism and constructive criticism. One is to insult you to the point where it could be emotional abuse and one is just advice on how to improve what you are saying or doing. Constructive criticism is obviously preferred. For instance, instead of telling someone they completely suck at singing, you could tell them that they just should consider checking into singing lessons to further improve their voice. You see, one goes much farther than the other. If you just simply insult someone and leave it at that, you can't expect them to get any better. If anything, they will get worse after hearing all the insults. It will build up in their mind and then they will ultimately believe that they truly aren't good at what they're doing. That's why constructive criticism is much more productive. As fellow humans, we are meant to work together and to build each other up and not tear each other down.

Ignoring all the hate that you get from other people (regardless of their relation to you), will save you a lot of emotional pain and turmoil. When you decide to go into submission and let others whip you with all of their rude comments, you begin to sell out and will lose sight of who you really are in the grand scheme of things. Stress will be abundant if you allow all of your haters and critics to beat you over the head with their thoughts and opinions. All of this will definitely make your life much more difficult than it may already be. Ignoring them can never be more wonderful to do when it comes to conflicts with other people trying to knock you down. Do your absolute best to stay clear from these kinds of people because they are nothing but bad news for you and your future. Make a point to constantly surround yourself with the people who want what is truly best for you and your interests. It's good to also understand that your interests may not be always what's best for you so it's definitely not a horrible idea to go ahead and take a few steps back so you can see how it could line up your destiny.

Spending time around the correct people who will lift you up and not tear you down is always what you will want whether your goals are good for your future life or not. Let's say that your goals aren't exactly the best for your future but you still want to do them anyway. This is where it gets tough for your loved ones who more than likely support you and you especially. Assuming your loved ones support you and your goals aren't the best for your future, they will likely give you helpful advice on what better paths to take instead of insulting you for going down the wrong path. Your family is your family and they know you better than anybody. Now if you were in a scenario where your goals do line up well with your future, then it would probably be better to get some constructive criticism from a good fellow friend because friends will most of the time be more straightforward with you while family members usually tend to sugarcoat the whole deal. While your family will still give you the right kind of criticism, they won't be as straightforward as would a friend.

Embracing what will make you advance in your interests is a very good feeling when you really get down to it. Sadly, not many people are willing to listen to what they need to learn and instead want to act before they think. You should always think before you speak and also listen before you speak. We all have two ears and one mouth for a reason. We were intended to use our ears more than our mouth. Humbling yourself to the point where you wish to learn from your mistakes and where you accept other people's advice to help build you up to become a better, stronger, more prepared, and all in all more successful is a life changing action. Ignoring all the rude, negative comments from others and focusing on learning from the people who build you up but also give you advice on how to overcome your flaws is also very life changing. It is perhaps, one of the best things you could ever do to self-improve yourself as a person.

Always disregard hate that tells you that you suck and that what you're doing is dumb, and welcome the love that tells you that you don't suck, but there's room for improvement.

Rule #18: Be the Change You Want to See

Change is something that we all seem to all hunger for every day. The more days that go by, the more we crave for a change in our life or maybe even just in the world in general. Regardless of where you want change, it's always something that we will constantly pursue - likely until we die. Of course, contentment is a must-have trait so you don't constantly lead a life full of nothing but dissatisfaction. Still though, there's absolutely nothing unethical or wrong with wanting change in the world unless you want bad change. Fortunately, very few people are for that kind of change. If you're stuck and don't know for sure how to bring about the change you're looking for, then it's best to first get to the root of the problem.

After figuring out the problem and thoroughly analyzing it, you can then decide to finally take the necessary actions to fully bring about that desired change you've longed for. Many people get caught up in the common myth which claims that one person isn't enough to bring about a change, much less any change at all. Luckily, this is far from being factual. All it takes to get the anchor off the ground is to start with you. You are enough to bring about change even if it's the slightest amount. No change is too small. Every single bit of small change is amazing for the world and will work its way to becoming a major change overtime which will positively cause a riptide against all the corruption that could be in your life and the entire world as a whole. For example, suppose one of your greatest, most loyal friends gets assaulted right before your eyes in an alleyway. It's no doubt a very horrible thing to witness, but it's not something you can just look at and walk away from without feeling any bit of guilt. It would be disloyal and disrespectful to leave a friend in need of support. That's why you have no choice but to take some sort of action to ensure that your friend won't be severely injured or killed. Whether that would be by getting help from a police officer or using force yourself, you need to do something. Or in a less serious scenario, you may see that somebody in a grocery store is in the checkout line and just remembered that he left his wallet at home and can't pay for his groceries. Well, you could do an act of kindness by choosing to pay for his items so he can be grateful and then would want to repay you. Remember though that in this situation and in many other situations like this, it's good to instead tell them to pay it forward to the next person and not to pay you back. The never-ending acts of kindness are the change that we all need to see much more of and can easily see more of if we allow it to happen. It's all up to us in the very end. We have as much power as we allow ourselves to all possess.

Have you ever seen anybody suffering with a disability that's so big that it could hinder their happiness and their whole quality of life? Many of us have. We all, to some degree, have a certain disability which can make it much more challenging to perform the tasks we wish. There is hope left in all of it though. Even if you are stuck with a major disability that prevents you from walking, you still can overcome it. It probably sounds corny in every fashion and even unrealistic. Sometimes what we believe is to be unrealistic though, isn't always unrealistic. What's considered far from realistic isn't impossible.

Ultimately, we all are only truly disabled by the limitations that we set for ourselves in our own minds. A disability is more of a mental belief and mental roadblock than it is a true disability. You can't ever give up just because someone told you one day that you can't walk right or you can't walk at all. You need to absorb every amount of confidence possible so you can fully take on all of the physical, mental, and emotional changes that await you on your goal. Nothing else will be as effective in making the change you want unless you step out of your comfort zone and face your fears. Don't fear making mistakes because that will always be how you learn and grow to become a better and stronger person. There's a bigger and better world out there that's waiting for you to simply take the first step and not be afraid to do some freefalling. Once you take the jump towards what you're hungering for, you will slowly see your parachute open. It doesn't happen right away and the journey can oftentimes look very frightening and critical, but it's always worth the risk. Not to mention, it is always worth the wait. The car ride to Change Avenue is typically a long, crooked one especially if you're seeking a major adjustment in the world. Don't ever let the path frighten you, but instead learn how to frighten it with your innate tenacity. Everybody has tenacity and all you need to do is let it out so you can shine bright to the opposition you face. As long as you are going all in with your sweat, blood, and tears, you will not find any force big enough to stop you from creating a positive change in the world.

Rule #19: Don't Fear Aging

The aging process is unquestionably frowned upon and even feared by many. When you get down to it, nobody actually likes getting older unless you're so young that you're itching to become a young adult. As people get to be in their thirties and up, they begin to realize that aging is taking somewhat of a toll on their looks and energy. This is typically when they begin to cringe and so the fear of aging begins.

Fear has dominated many aspects of people's lives and prevents them from usually doing what they are passionate about. For instance, if somebody really was big on modeling and wanted to be a model, but thought they weren't model material because they're a little up there in age and so they decided to opt out. This specific scenario is what makes most potential models fail because they don't even bother trying in the first place. Not only will fear of age affect your possible modeling opportunities, but could affect other areas of your life. Certain people (although not many) are literally afraid to step foot outside of their doorstep because they are afraid that people may look at them with disgust, due to how much they may have aged. Situations like this are pretty severe and can put a quick damper on your quality of life, specifically your social life. You can either choose to be a slave to fear or you can choose to break the chains and live a healthier and more fulfilling life. There's nothing more tragic than being a prisoner to what you are afraid of. The chances of you ever progressing in your life are zero if you decide to stay in submission day in and day out. Nobody but you can prevent you from facing this ugly tragedy.

You are frankly as young as you carry yourself. For example, you could walk, talk, and act very immature or you could decide to walk like a respectable citizen, talk appropriately, and act towards situations with manners. Not to mention, you can control how young you look by getting enough rest, taking supplements, exercising, etc. There's truly no limit on how well you can take care of yourself so you can be looking fresh and young. With knowing all this, it should dramatically encourage you to want to finally give up the fear that you may have about aging. Aging isn't all a bad thing either. Just like there are pros and cons to everything in life, there's also pros and cons to aging itself. As you age you do tend to look older, but you become more knowledgeable and the longer you are living, the neater experiences you will encounter. Just imagine how many wonderful things there are to witness in your lifetime. There's just way too much to see in this world to the point where it's overwhelming! While that is irritating, it is also a plus because there's always something new you can see and you will never get tired of what you can all see all throughout life. There's countless countries to visit, plenty of oceans to sightsee and swim in, and numerous lakes to fish in. The possibilities for a splendid, fulfilling life are endless! The only limits that we have in this life are the ones that we set for ourselves. Oftentimes, we tend to think the exact opposite and believe that we have limits that we can never get past. The word aging itself is a limitation for mankind. When someone hears that they aged they automatically are fearful. You don't want to just be another victim. Realize that aging can be a good thing and get out and start living life!

This may sound crazy, but some people are so fearful of aging that they will avoid laughing or smiling. The simple act of smiling or laughing is known to eventually give people laugh lines or wrinkles but if you avoid laughing and having a good time because you're afraid this will cause aging. What kind of life is that? Life wasn't meant to be lived in total darkness and fear. It's meant to be enjoyed and lived to the fullest. Besides, laughing and smiling provides a bunch of positive benefits for the human body. For one, it will boost your immune system and will allow you to live longer and better. Your quality of life depends on your mood and how you choose to react to situations. If you prefer to be sad and upset over being joyful, then you will no doubt lead a lower quality of life. The reasons for why you should be of a joyful spirit and not fear aging go on forever. Aside from it just helping you live better and longer, it also will make you a more triumphant person when it comes to your goals. Not only that, but it will just help you become more victorious as a person in general. For example, you will naturally have more energy to get daily tasks done that need attention. So, what's stopping you? Turn that frown upside down, share some laughs with close friends and family members, and cheat your fear of aging. Your fear will no longer be present once you demand it to leave. Get out of submission and begin your transition to greatness!

Rule #20: Put in More Work to Get More Out

If you put good in, then you get good out. Right? Right. You can never expect to get fantastic results from your work if you don't do the work well or if you don't do enough of it. Work is not valued as much as it should be these days. Many people even go as far as to want the results far before the work. That just doesn't work. You can't ever put the cart before the horse. Instead, you have no choice but to first do the work and then see your results unfold. Understand that just doing the work though first isn't enough. You need to make sure that you also are working endlessly for your passion.

When you want something bad enough you will do or give just about anything to get it. Desperation is a very common feeling for people when they want to achieve their difficult goals. Many people will tell you that the only reason some of these celebrities are where they're at is because they had enormous amounts of luck. That is debatable, but if you really wrap your head around it, it's not exactly luck that got them there. It's either connections or themselves. The only time one is really lucky in their endeavors is when they grind, grind, and grind.

Whether you are grinding for outstanding connections or just working your tail off in other ways, it is always grind. The harder and longer you work, the luckier you get. So, don't let anybody fool you with the idea that all these successful people got to where they're at just because they 'got lucky'.

Every day that passes you should be sweating, panting, and bleeding. Well, not literally...but you should be giving it your all, all the time. You don't have to be so extreme to the point where you set unrealistic expectations for yourself in impossible amounts of time, but make sure you at least set appropriate goals for yourself everyday so that you are able to follow through with your goals and hold yourself fully accountable. Let's assume that you want to type out some of your book every day, but don't always have enough time to do it. It would be wise to first get up earlier, eat breakfast, and then focus on only typing out a page a day so that you aren't working on too much of your book or too little. This works even for the busiest of people.

If you are trying to get more work done, but you can't seem to remember where you left off then it may not be a bad idea to leave some 'footprints' for yourself so you can pick up from your stopping point. There's nothing more frustrating than trying to remember where you stopped working. This can especially be a major time-killer that will leave you not only annoyed with not knowing where to pick up where you originally left off, but you will also turn your eyes to the clock and notice that much more of your day has been chewed up for good. Always make a point to leave some marks so that you don't have to go through the hassle. It is worth the extra couple of minutes to leave footprints instead of wasting a half an hour or possibly more!

Getting more done is an excellent thing to do, but many think this means that they should start multitasking. While multitasking seems like it would be a wonderful option to take in completing tasks, it is actually the polar opposite.

Multitasking is a waste of time and work. Of course, you want to work harder for what you desire, but multitasking is never a good way to get there. Working more intensely doesn't mean that you should do more work at once, it just means that you should work harder at one specific task at a time. Not to mention, after each task that you work fiercely at, you want to then give yourself a small break to take in some fresh air.

It may seem like most of your work if not all of it is all for nothing. When you continuously do something, you won't always get the results right away. It doesn't matter how long and how hard you push for something that you really desire; you still will end up waiting awhile for results or at least this typically is the case. Patience is not just important to have and maintain, but also, it's very important to have when you are working for hours and hours on what you are trying to achieve. Patience and hard work combine very well and they both are some of the few main keys to success in your life. Without patience your efforts won't be as big because when you don't have the tolerance to wait you get disappointed easier and then when you try to work for your passion under disappointment, it is so much more challenging. Always keep your tolerance level as high as possible.

Distractions are too common in our society. It seems like there's a distraction around every corner. Interferences will play with your life and try to catch you off guard left and right. This is when you want a low tolerance level. You want to make sure to never tolerate background noise as it just prevents you from getting down to business. Don't let yourself become distracted because you will ultimately become trapped. Once you're trapped, it's hard to break free from the distraction that caught you. Be bigger than your distractions, be smarter than your distractions, stay focused, and never stop working hard.

Rule #21: Don't Live to Work, Work to Live

Work, as we know, it is usually boring and tiresome. It's not something people truly ever want to do and only seem to do it because they have to. Work is sometimes underrated, but can also be extremely overrated as well. These people are known as workaholics and never want to take even a few short breaks from work. This is not at all something that you should ever consider doing. The list goes on and on for why you should never become a workaholic. It's just another trap that many of us fall into.

Many individuals feel that if they work endlessly without a single break that they will accomplish not only more, but will simply have a better and brighter future for themselves and their family. Unfortunately, this is never really the case. Workaholics who never stop working may get more done, but they won't have a brighter future nor will their families. Neglect for the family is usually what comes out of scenarios where the dad or mom don't take breaks from their job. It's a tragedy in itself and is not at all a good thing. Family is always supposed to be valued far before a job. Somewhere along the way though people got this mixed up and can't seem to ever arrange their priorities in the correct manner. This is when families fall apart and this is when your success will fall apart to. You may be progressing with your career or possibly your dream job, but you will be regressing with your family. Without your family, your life is not as meaningful and is doomed to fall apart. Make sure to keep your priorities in the correct manner. Setting up your priorities properly is always a top priority!

Understand that you don't have to go to the other extreme either where you literally stop working and don't work at all. The point is to not overwork. Think of yourself like a battery. You need to recharge yourself just like a battery needs to be recharged after so much use. Not only does overworking cause you to drain your energy, but it will make you much unhealthier as a person. Not only will it drain you physically, but also mentally and emotionally.

You can't lead a normal and stable life with an unhealthy mind. Your health is your everything as is your family too. Without your health and your family what good is life? You could have all of the money in the entire world, but if you don't have your health or family to take care of you when you're sick then your life is going to fail. Even when you aren't sick, it's always a blessing to have your family around to spend time with.

Never live to work, but work to live. You have to make a living somehow and you should definitely have some career to make that happen, but you don't need to work your entire life away. Your life is precious and every single moment that you inhale and exhale is also just as precious so why work until you have nothing left of you? It's unfortunate that many people find out the hard way. Normally, people don't ever know what they have until it's totally gone. That's why it's important to cherish every single breathing moment while it lasts because you can count on it being gone.

You will likely regret all of the vacations you could have taken with your family and friends. Not to mention, you probably will regret doing just about anything else if you decided to do nothing but work your whole life away. A life full of regrets isn't a life worth living. This is the harsh reality for work addicts. A job was never intended to take your whole life and soul away from you. It was instead meant to provide you an income.

A great way to prevent from falling into the trap of becoming a work addict is to choose a workplace that meets your needs. It's a wonderful idea to ask current employed workers to see if their work-life balance is in check or not. If it's not, then kindly go on to the next business. Checking reviews for businesses and even talking to the manager about your expectations will help give you an idea if the job is right for your life or not.

Aside from neglecting family and such, there are plenty of other signs that occur when you decide to lead a life geared fully towards work and nothing else. Some other signs include neglecting your own health. Sadly, many chase wealth over their health. While they may want their health, they focus more on getting wealthy than staying healthy. For example, they would prefer to work their whole day away, every single day just to get a bigger check. More money is always a wonderful thing, but it's never ever worth sacrificing your own health just to get ahead financially. Wealth is not health. It can definitely help make you healthier, but wealth itself is never health. Health is wealth. Health is everything in your life and it shouldn't ever be viewed as a minor thing.

An even better example for how putting work first in your life is bad is if someone were to work without breaks, never take care of their hygiene, neglect their families, and constantly eat junk food and then end up with a sudden heart attack right as they get their big check. This is the trap that you want to avoid like the plague! It's nice to get bigger checks, but what good would that check be if you were severely injured or on your deathbed. Even if the check was worth a million dollars or more it wouldn't make a difference. Without your proper health, you will never be able to enjoy the benefits of having lots of money. Working to live will put you into situations like this. It can't be stressed enough, when you choose work over everything else your life is always going to be out of sync. Just be careful in your walk of life and always keep an eye out for your work-life balance. Think of this work-life balance as if it were literally a scale. You never want a scale to be unbalanced not even by a little bit. Instead, you want to maintain the scale and keep it completely balanced.

Rule #22: Have Lots of Faith

Doubt is, no doubt, a dream killer for us all. The moment doubt invades our life is the moment our life begins to fall apart. With doubt comes anxiety and frustration and all of this can lead to a sad end to one's dreams for their future.

Whether you doubt that you can do what you want or have what you want, it all is negative energy that eats away all of your hope. Don't make the same common mistake many make when they chase their aspirations.

There are many things you can do to prevent yourself from being in constant doubt with the things in your life. You first need to believe in yourself before anything or anybody else. You need to take care of yourself before anything or anyone else otherwise you won't know the meaning of who you are as a person.

You basically need to 'find yourself' before doing anything else. Maybe consider traveling to another country or you could go somewhere as simple as your local state park. The point is to do anything to get away from your normal routine so you can see who you really are. Over time you will begin to realize that you are much better than you think you are as a person.

Learning to stick to a habit regardless of how much criticism you get is a great idea. The only time you ever want to let in criticism in your personal life is when it's to help you improve and not to emotionally hurt you. All other criticism should be disregarded. Staying committed to your goals and having faith in yourself will always be in your best interest. While you're at it, it's not a bad idea to set higher goals. Setting higher standards can be frightening though as you are required to do more than you originally planned for yourself. The thing to do is to remain trustful throughout the difficult times even when it seems like everything's falling apart. It's easy for a person to feel good and remain positive when things are going smooth, but when things start getting shaky is when your faith truly comes in. Your faith is based on trusting that everything will be alright even when things in your life are showing otherwise. When all else fails, have faith. It couldn't be more straightforward than that.

This may sound totally out of the ordinary and even insane, but a great way to exercise your faith is to welcome rejection at your doorstep. Putting yourself out there whether you get rejected or not is a great thing! If you never get out and take risks, then you will never get anywhere. Basically, if you are just going to keep aiming for nothing, then that's what you will get. Never see rejection as a bad thing and never run away from the chances of becoming a victim to it. It's much, much better to be victim to rejection than a slave to fear. Go out and make mistakes! Don't be robotic and act like you aren't allowed to make even one single mistake. You are human! You are allowed to mess up and then go back and fix it. The awesome thing about messing up is that you can get the chance to improve it and then look back at how much you improved. If you had nothing to polish about yourself, then think about how boring life would be. Perfect is boring! Everybody wants to be perfect, but don't bother trying. You're just fine the way you are. Maybe tweak a few things here and there to better yourself, but by the end of the day, you are enough! If you are always chasing the wind you will never be happy. Have faith in yourself that you can accomplish great things!

Positive views are always blocks that help build your faith. A fantastic way to further a positive self-image is to look back at all of your past achievements. Not only should you think about all the wonderful things you have done, but also write them down. It may sound unnecessary and a complete time waster, yet, it's much more powerful than you think. As you write down all of your accomplishments, you will begin to see that there are certain things you've done well time and time again. This is what you are gifted at. What you specialize in is what you probably enjoy doing. Never minimize how powerful it is when you write down all of your previous successes.

Spending time around those that love and care about you will also strengthen your faith immensely. It's true that they may sugarcoat certain things about you as they never intend to hurt your feelings, but in the end, they just want to see you succeed. So, whenever you feel down on your luck and you believe that you are failing at basically everything, ask a close friend or family member what they think you are good at. Also, be sure to tell them that you want an honest answer that isn't exaggerated. While you want an encouraging answer, you still want them to be blunt. Take any advice from them even if you think if may be small and unimportant. Any bit of additional advice is wonderful no matter how big or small. As long as you learn from a loved one on how to improve your chances of reaching your goals, you will begin to see your faith in yourself grow.

Taking proper care of yourself is just another excellent way to keep strong faith in yourself. First, you want to make sure to keep your hygiene and appearance in check. Allow yourself enough time every day to shower, brush your teeth, and shave any facial hair if needed. Next, you want to eat on a healthy basis. This will not only further enhance your appearance, but it will also just make you feel better physically and emotionally. Additionally, you want to exercise daily or at least four times a week so you can get the benefits of feeling happier and so much more!

Finally, it's in your best interest to get enough sleep each night to ensure that you can perform at your best for daily tasks and so that you can feel better about yourself. By following all of this you will see a huge increase in the faith you have for yourself. Don't stop believing and most importantly, don't stop believing in you.

Rule #23: Obsess with Success

The vision for success can be a very bright and positive one. It can also undoubtedly be a very dark and negative one. Your outlook and drive for any specific victory you want to attain is entirely up to you. If you want to do something bad enough you will likely have a racing mind to the point where you find yourself tossing and turning in bed. As much as this is a bad thing, it is also a good thing too believe it or not. When you think about your goals and the risks you need to take it could possibly cause you to temporarily mess up. It will even make you anxious. Basically, if you're not anxious and struggling, then your goals are not big enough. If you're not obsessed in what you're pursuing, then you probably need a whole different aspiration to work towards. Obsession is the key to succession! Without obsession, your drive towards what you were working at will be clearly low.

There are many ways to get successful. Many that will get you to certain places in your life you weren't necessarily at to start with, yet, they only seem to get you so far. There's truly only one set way to become a triumphant person. Unfortunately, it's not stressed enough to the general public leaving them wasting their full potential. The only surefire way to release your full potential is to be obsessed. The human mind is certainly very powerful. This happens to be an understatement though. We don't give our brains the recognition it deserves and this limits our abilities as a result. Obsession is seen as a negative word and is sometimes linked to certain mental disorders, but it's also a good thing too.

Unhealthy fixations are very real, but so are healthy fixations. Just because you fixate on something doesn't for sure mean it is a bad fixation.

You may not be at a point in your life right now where you know exactly what to fixate on and that's okay. It's best to take it one day at a time and continue to seek what you are really interested in. Once you do find your passion, the obsession will then begin to naturally occur. Once the obsession is alive in you, don't back down! Just because you may then have found your passion doesn't mean it will stay alive in you unless you feed the fire. You must continue to add fuel to the fire otherwise that fire will begin to go out. Sadly, once the fire is gone, it's tough to get it back. Don't be afraid to have a fixation when it's a good one. Keep in mind to that it's a great idea to also find more obsessions for your life that will not only benefit you but also others as well.

You will begin a follower in this world but will transition to becoming a leader. More specifically, you will become a leader of what you're pursuing whether it's art, songwriting, teaching, etc. Obsession helps you improve and eventually even master your craft. With strong desire comes strong motivation and with strong motivation comes strong results. The sad thing is many people prefer to live paycheck to paycheck just because it's an easier and more stable way of living. Easier and better are two entirely different things though. You must always remember this to keep yourself from falling prey to mediocrity.

If there is one thing you can do to prevent yourself from being unsuccessful it is to never ever settle. Even when you think you have made fantastic progress, don't decide to stop there. You will always be selling yourself short if you decide to get comfortable and settle. Life begins at the end of your comfort zone. You have to be comfortable with obsessing at your dreams. If you finally decide to obsess, then you will begin to notice that you can accomplish anything. Success will never openly come to you; you have to go to it. It's basically the red x and will never be found unless you seek it.

You may have wondered time and time again about how you could get focused and stay obsessed with what you love. Fortunately, there are countless ways that can help you stay interested in pursuing your set dreams. One way is if you have a phone or a computer you could have your background be of all your obsessions. This allows you to constantly be reminded of the goals that you have at stake so you don't forget them or lose interest. It's just one excellent way to embed your passions deep into your mind!

Another way would be to get a calendar if you don't already have one, so you can plan every little and big detail about what you will do for each day. This will not only help you plan things out to help you get closer to your objectives, but it will also reduce any stress that could have been built up due to lack of planning.

Next, would be to take a glance at your social circle to see who you all are connected with. You should find most, if not all, nice and supportive people in your social circle. If you happen to notice that there are even a few unsupportive people that you are connected to, then it's best to either completely disconnect from them or at the very least drastically limit your communication with them. There's nothing worse than being around people who constantly knock you down. You have two choices: you can either allow yourself to hang around people who constantly tear you down and then get so discouraged to the point where you just throw in the towel and quit or you can choose to disconnect or at least limit your time around discouraging people and instead spend time around uplifting people who will make you want to be a winner and not a quitter. When you begin to hang around the right people who are there to build you up, then you will keep your healthy obsessions strong. For the record, the only obsessions that will be kept strong if you hang around negative people are the unhealthy ones. You become who you surround yourself with so surround yourself wisely. Stay around positive people and you will constantly see a growth in your healthy obsessions for victory. Obsess, obsess, obsess! Don't bother stressing thinking about all of your problems when you could be obsessing over the solutions to which will then lead you to the gates of victory!

Rule #24: Excuse the Excuses

If there's one thing that many people do it's making excuses. It seems when everybody is in a sticky situation they feel as if making any excuse possibly will get them out of their problems. This may temporarily work for a while, but in the end, you will find that you will begin to show your true colors to others. If you have to make an excuse every time you get in a difficult situation, then it will make you appear very irresponsible for your actions and you will certainly be viewed as a dependent person to the outside world. This is something you don't want to fall prey to. The faster you excuse your excuses, the better responsible you will be for your own actions.

Making excuse after excuse will limit your chances of any sort of success that society has to offer. This is because people won't want to work with anyone who constantly has to justify themselves. It's alright to justify yourself now and then, but there's a point where you can get extreme and go overboard. Sometimes you have no choice but to own your errors by apologizing for what you messed up on. Everybody can and will mess up through the course of their lives and you are no different. We all make mistakes, but it's up to us if we choose to own our errors or totally disregard them and act like we are never wrong. It's okay to be wrong!

It's not wrong to be wrong. You should allow yourself room for error so then you will have the humility to fix your problems. Don't excuse your humility! Excuse your excuses. Your humility will be basically nonexistent if you can never keep yourself from making excuses for everything you mess up on.

If you look at the vast majority of the successful people today and take a look back at their history, then you will probably notice that they didn't make excuses or at least very rarely. Excuses will always keep you from going all out and releasing your full potential. Always! Not to mention, making excuses is just another way of procrastinating. They are literally one in the same. Procrastinating and making all these reasons will get you absolutely nowhere at all. You can't be afraid to fail and even when you do mess up (because you will), you still can't give up. Remember, you don't actually fail until you quit for good. Sadly, if you have an urge to make excuses and can't quit the urge, then you will have a very low chance of wanting to still pursue what you desire. For example, if you're working towards becoming a bodybuilder and want to hit the gym soon, but feel a little tired, then you will likely want to make an excuse to not go to the fitness center and instead lay on the couch which will then set you back with your goals and make you closer to quitting for good. This is what excuses do for a person. It restricts them from getting to where they should be. It's a trap that you must avoid at all costs.

Sometimes having a support system can help you stay motivated in your aspirations rather than causing you to want to make reasons for why you don't want to continue your grind. Before you have your ideal support system, you must be sure to go out and find it. Don't rush the process when you begin to look for the friends you need. Keep in mind that this is serious business and that your entire future will depend on it. While you want someone who's nice you don't want them to be too nice. If you choose friends to be the coaches for you, then make sure that they won't be afraid to give you good constructive criticism so that you can grow from any faults you may have.

Once you manage to find at least a good few friends that will keep you in line, your journey will be much less challenging and just life in general will become more hopeful. For best results, it's great to find a few friends who share the same interests as you so that they will be even more motivated themselves to want to help keep you motivated. Of course, friends who have different interests from you still can help keep you on track, yet they likely won't be as interested in helping you. Most importantly, make sure they're not feeling down on their luck and confirm if they are doers or not. If they are not doers themselves, then you can't at all expect any bit of help from them. You need someone who has a focused mind and who isn't afraid to tackle each goal that they set.

Once you have your small support system in place, it may not be a terrible idea to go all out and grow your support system further. There is strength in numbers and the more people you have helping you stay focused the better. Think of it like this: the more people you have supporting you, the less excuses you will ever even think of making. Another win to having more people in your support system is not only will you get more help more often, but you will also be able to help anybody in your network as well. Excuses will never triumph over you especially when you equip yourself with a large network of people who will coach you and who you can coach as well in the fight against making justifications.

Justifications or excuses will only delay you from getting the golden trophy. You may be closer to getting your ultimate prize than you probably think, but it's the actions you take is what determines exactly how much closer you will get to finally getting the grand prize. It's pretty simple: all you need to do is throw away the excuses and make improvements on yourself so you can then progress further to reaching your objectives for good. You can do this! You can become stronger and smarter than your excuses. You are in control and nobody else. Don't wait, excuse the excuses!

Rule #25: Don't Be Confined by Your Rules

As beneficial as having rules are you need to also learn to not get too wrapped up in having a set of rules. Rule setting can make you or break you. Without rules, your life will automatically be a mess so don't ever think that you must go with no rules at all. Instead, still be sure to allow rules in your life but just not too many. In other words, don't have a rule for every single thing you do. If you go down the path of having rules for everything, then you will be seen as extremely abnormal to the outside world and you will simply be an unhappy person all around.

Rules were never meant to restrict you from enjoying a nice, fulfilling life. They were meant to actually help you live an organized, yet happy life. Organization isn't bad unless it's done to the extreme. Then again, everything becomes a bad thing if done to the extreme. The key is moderation. You want to assure that your life is balanced, but not too balanced. You can determine if you want a balanced, unbalanced, or extreme life. Having an extreme lifestyle of tight rules is basically just as bad as having an unorganized lifestyle with no rules whatsoever.

Ultimately, if you must break a rule here and there just to feel normal then go ahead and do it. It may sound like a wrong idea to break any specific rule, but it's not always the worst thing in the world. There are plenty of even worse things out there. It's better to break a rule every now and then versus never breaking any rule and having a very unhappy life. Your happiness matters much more! For instance, if you must eat unhealthily for a couple of days and break your rule of clean eating then so be it. You must treat yourself sometimes.

You can't expect to be perfect and never mess up. Not only will you accidentally break certain rules but you will probably break a couple rules on purpose. This isn't exactly a good thing, but it's not always a bad thing. Rules weren't only meant to be followed, but they were also meant to be broken under certain circumstances. This may sound absolutely ridiculous, but it couldn't hold more truth. You see, when you constantly follow rules and never allow yourself to break one, you not only make yourself more likely to be unhappy but also you restrict yourself from learning. Whether you break rules on purpose or on accident, there is always a lesson to be learned right after.

There are several additional reasons why you shouldn't always feel like you have to follow every single rule out there. One very great one happens to be that rules are not universal. Some rules fit more people than others, but not every rule is always necessary to follow. Some rules just aren't adjusted for your own self. So, it would be foolish to have any rules to follow that don't fit you.

Another reason is that you become more independent and not as dependent upon orders that others may have set before you. This may sound strange, but you can actually become dependent upon your own rules and then slowly lose your own identity. This scenario can be just as bad as becoming dependent upon other people's rules. Again, rules should be followed but not to the point where you begin to lose sight of who you are. A good rule of thumb is if there's any rule out there that causes you to question who you are as a person or just makes you feel out of place in any way, then simply ignore it or even break it.

Breaking the rules is practically always seen as a mischievous act in society, but it's not always what it seems. In fact, breaking the rules and questioning society is sometimes the best thing that could ever happen to our civilization. A lot of the advancements that have occurred in our medicine and technology was because people questioned society! Don't get brainwashed into thinking that second guessing anything is bad. If we had more thinkers and less followers who would stand up for their thoughts and not the mainstream ideas of the world, then we would see massive improvements in our world.

If it means having your own identity and not becoming a mindless, walking, talking zombie where you feel like you have to follow every rule that society has, then it's worth breaking some rules here and there. Don't feel like you have to follow every rule or any rule that makes you feel unsure of yourself. Be yourself and not what the world wants. You may have a brain just like anybody else, but not the same brain. Everybody thinks differently. While certain people do think alike, they still do think different from each other. You don't need to follow what everybody else is doing one hundred percent of the time, nor should they feel that way about you. It pays to be independent!

At the end of it all, don't be afraid to live life and be who you truly are. Living is what makes life, well, life and you are what makes you, you. Don't let any particular rule determine who you are as a person. It's a wonderful thing to be able to have structure in your life but never let your rule setting become who you are. If you allow rules to steal your identity, then that's where your happiness ends. Keep your identity and happiness, but still allow yourself to have some rules. Verify that they are reasonable and not over the top so that you can not only live a life full of structure, but you can also live a life full of happiness, and then one day you will be able to stand up in your later years and acknowledge that you were able to have set rules which allowed you to rule successfully.

www.ingramcontent.com/pod-product-compliance
Lightning Source LLC
Chambersburg PA
CBHW071423040426
42445CB00012BA/1279